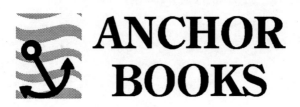

ANCHOR BOOKS

CELTIC CONNECTION

Edited by

Sarah Andrew

First published in Great Britain in 2001 by
ANCHOR BOOKS
Remus House,
Coltsfoot Drive,
Peterborough, PE2 9JX
Telephone (01733) 898102

HB ISBN 1 85930 931 3
SB ISBN 1 85930 936 4

FOREWORD

Anchor Books is a small press, established in 1992, with the aim of promoting readable poetry to as wide an audience as possible.

We hope to establish an outlet for writers of poetry who may have struggled to see their work in print.

The poems presented here have been selected from many entries. Editing proved to be a difficult task and as the Editor, the final selection was mine.

I trust this selection will delight and please the authors and all those who enjoy reading poetry.

Sarah Andrew
Editor

CONTENTS

STRANGE SHOES

Brown eyes open in wonder
as I told you stories
while you sat upon my knee . . .
Now I stare at you in wonder . . .
Gone the fat little legs
running around the garden
chasing ducks and hens
and hiding in home-made dens
always a bruised forehead from
too many falls off your bicycle . . .
Now you have long skinny legs
that dance the night away
in enormous strange shoes
balanced by unusually weird
yet somehow fascinating hairstyles . . .
I watch in amazement
and admire all your braveness
           that I never had . . .
You zoom through your young life
in carefree haste busily collecting
tattoos and assorted friends along the way . . .
Brown eyes wide open in wonder . . .
Now covered in fancy make-up
Now covered in complicated plans
           and important ideas
You never seem to show any fears . . .
Brown eyes wide open in wonder . . .

Netta Irvine

RAMELTON

A soft veil of rain drifts over the bay.
From the Salmon-House to Market Square
The steep brae glistens with the slime
And scale of fish oil
                that has seeped
From high-cribbed lorries, hauling the early-morning
Catch from Rathmullen to Greencastle.
At the quay fishing boats bob and creak
As they strain against
                tyre cushioned moorings.
Yellow ochre, orange, light brown, copper coloured
Leaves are cast from tall trees into the River Lennon.
They fuse to form a giant patchwork-quilt, a magic-carpet
Mosaic that is carried by a current that bubbles
                and ripples over
Weed-draped riverbed rocks as it makes its way
Towards Lough Swilly. The dawn chorus of wild finches
Comes alive, then falls silent as a bird of prey
Floats high above the landscape. From reed beds
                in the distance
A curlew's mournful cry rises and stirs thoughts
Of home from within me. The sights and sounds
Of Ramelton will come to me often. As I travel
Homewards my heart feels like a flower: pressed
                between two pages.

John Michael Doherty

GOING POTTY

I'm a great lover of clay,
My sister exclaims, 'Clay?'
'Yes,' I say with vigour, 'Clay!'
It's so adaptable, so inviting.
You begin and think, 'What now?'
Suddenly an idea forms,
and away you go.
My friends say, 'You must be
running out of space by now.'
But somehow I find a place
for each wee treasure.
Oh, that waiting for the biscuit firing,
- wondering 'Has it popped?'
But no - there is your wee
masterpiece in the making.
Then to choose the appropriate
glazes - that's so important.
And the time it takes to do it
meticulously.
Then the final glazing and
- Oh, you're aghast!
What a joy to belong to a
super pottery class.

Dorothy Allen

How Rich Am I

What an interesting life I lead
So many things I want and need
I want to be a millionaire
Or at least to have my fair share
I want to drive a big fast car
To travel near and travel far
Every day my life is just the same
I want the money and the fame
I do the lottery every Saturday night
Wishing some day to get it right
Fly to London, Paris and Rome
New York could be my home
No more worries about tomorrow
Never have to beg or even borrow
But then there are people worse off than me
The comforts I have they will never see.
So tonight when I kneel and pray
It's for them poor souls far away.

Paul O'Boyle

DANCE IN THE SUN

O to be a child,
To sing in the rain
Dance in the sun
To pick wild flowers
In the wind
To walk in the park
Where little bird sings
To smile when
The sweet snow
Falls in my eyes
To cry when the lamb
That's shy
Seems lost for a while.

Helen Owen

TREES

In the light summer breeze,
Trees they dance and sway,
Casting off their leaves,
When autumn,
Calls the day.

When winter's face,
It's time to show,
The same are packed,
With deepened snow.

Springtime comes
To renew,
Trees old,
And help the young,
Grow strong and bold.

Damian Begley

COCOONED
(To my grandson Charles Robert born 1st October 1998)

This cocoon has been dark and warm
Decide to escape to the outside world.
Along a winding canal to find a way out
Long hard struggle; see a chink of light.
Sound of voices had all been a hum
Bright lights, now upside down hung.
A protest yell, don't like what I found
Two strong, loving arms hold me tight
A soothing hand caresses my cheek
Warm lips plant a kiss upon my brow
Perhaps this world won't be so bad
I'm the third child in this family now.

Frances Joan Crawford

THE HEALING

Hope fades as waning moon
without the steady sustenance
of good-fortuned circumstance
and, as it dwindles, countenance
spurns smiling all too soon.

Heal me with your laughing eyes
which sorrow's welts will cauterise
with their tender warmth.

Perry McDaid

LIFE BEGINS AT 60

I'd thought 'being oldish' meant nothing to do
Eventually unfulfilled I've arrived at this stage too.
My family grown up and I've given them my best
I now choose to be active and perhaps later a rest.

I slowly adapted with full support from my care
Now when needed I'm not always there.
It's sometimes a case of hide and seek
How I wish there were more days in a week.

I made contact with friends, we exchanged views
We commenced weekly walking - we had nothing to lose.
Our lifestyle took an unexpected twist
Soon we had swimming, golfing and line dancing on our list.

An introduction to Bridge, at first hard to grasp
Influenced by players who adapted our task
A run through computers, stimulating the mind
Renewed fresh confidence, tedious dullness left behind.

Courses in First Aid, Calligraphy to add but a few
Abundance of new friends in all that we do.
We achieved many things we thought out of reach
And long past activities we can now teach.

With my dancing experience I pass on to my lot
They are pleased and surprised at the knowledge I've got
Age doesn't matter - it's the precious time we share
With friends and companions and families who care.

Kathleen McBrien

WHAT PRICE LOVE?

Brought together in a country full of hate,
The couple knew death would be their fate,
Fear, torment and intimidation,
Made their lives nothing but a damnation.

Why couldn't they leave them alone?
Let them stay in their marital home,
What have they done to deserve their pain?
They loved each other, that would always remain.

Piles upon piles of threatening letters came,
The terrorist thugs showed no shame,
The woman was found murdered in bed,
The husband received a bullet to his head.

What benefits from this act,
Is not found on any Bible tract,
The hatred still remains here,
And will go on for many a year.

Stop the fighting and the pain,
Let us all live in the one domain,
Peaceful together with love for all,
Living in hope that another war won't befall.

Pamela Craig

MY UTOPIA

Blue crushed velvet waters spread out over the horizon
Splashes of silver swirls materialise periodically
Sunrise, colour transforms, an ocean of wonderment
Evolves before me

I always loved the sea,
The colours, the rage, the calmness.
A bit like life.
Sometimes peaceful, maybe rocky.

A place to think, a place to dream
By the shore, alone, happy, content
A place where life stops and dreams take over
Stress leaves my soul, tranquillity takes over

The soft breeze changes mood
The sea accompanies her
The silver swirls become white, angry twists
My mood never falters

This is where I belong
Beside the sea
My home, my preserver
My Utopia.

Liz Johnston

APPRECIATE LIFE

I looked at the buttercups and daisies
I heard a blackbird sing
The fragrance of the roses filled the air
A butterfly flew by with multicoloured wing.

The bumblebee hummed a merry tune
As he gathered pollen from the flowers
Raindrops shone like diamonds
On grass so fresh from the showers.

Children laughing merrily
Dipping their warm toes in the cool stream
Lovers pass by, hand in hand
Hoping to find their dream.

Birds soar high above fluffy white clouds
Across a sky of azure blue
If you stop, look and listen
These things will bring contentment to you.

Elizabeth Collins

An Old Man's Companion

An old man walked his stick
across Thomond Bridge today.
I saw his hazel companion
smartly tap his boot.
I saw it poke the litter
to one well organised side.
Was he looking for something?
Money. I had spent mine!

He watched the swans gliding
in the river.
White and perfect and
from a distance
he watched two fishermen
catch nothing and
thought life is short
when you have lived it.
Then he walked
his stick back home
alone.

Marie Coghlan

HEAVEN

Heaven is a special place
on earth, where east, north, south
and west agree. It always
brings good harvest and
there the heard is always at home.

And at heaven's gate; where the golden
hearts are found, over heaven's gate
are arms of love for those unfound.

At three times daily heaven calls
out to Castle, town and people
Roses bloom joy and goodwill remain
in that special corner called heaven.

Brian Wolohan

To My - One True Love

Every day I think of you
Longing to be near,
your sweet, sweet heart
and sweet, sweet voice
and everything that's dear.

I wish that you were here with me
every single day,
kissing me
and hugging me,
and never were away.

I can't get you out of my head
however hard I try.
I think of you more and more
as each day
passes by.

I have your mobile number,
but I am scared to call,
just in case you reject me
that would just
make me fall.

One day I will have the courage,
to stand up and tell the truth,
but that day has
yet to dawn
I'm going through the roof.

Jennifer Miller

SORE AFFLICTED

I've some music in my soul,
    For a few words here and there;
Is there a need to listen,
    From some folk I know not where?

The tunes they never go away,
    'Less hard you try too much,
Then wither they like morning mist
    When the sun's rays get to touch.

But come they back like madness,
    What do they want with me?
To make me dance when I would rest
    And hear their symphony.

Is it music in its soul,
    Makes the blackbird sing so sweet?
Is there music in a moonbeam
    When it lands down at your feet?

The words they only follow
    What's around us all the time,
And mercy for that little tune,
    That at times the words they find.

Alistair McLean

BEACHES

Beaches now are circumscribed. Not like when we
Moved along the margin of love's new shoreline
Proffering as infinite sky and water,
sun and horizon.

Blue but clouded, slivers of razor shells and
sky, long hauled by breakers, aligned before us,
sandman, woman, grateful for dream gifts, gift dreams,
Shell crunching, beaching.

Waves, retreating, murmured, salaamed, and we were
sky clasped, sun snagged, prisoners love bound, kite high.
Oyster catchers, jealously, grubbed at sand pools,
narked to be outwinged.

Beaches now are circumscribed. Concrete sea walls,
winter sand dunes, calendar blank days, absence.
High tide flaunts its affluence; its detritus
tangled with riches.

Low tide jumble's hopelessly stalled: the lobster
pot which snares the kite string; the eggshell azure
stones; the sun and sea wind flayed tree trunk, stranded,
harbouring grudges.

Love, whichever sheltering shore you walk on,
feel with me the limitless wind which sculpts all
sandbars, hear the ebb tide which, dying, sapphic,
whispers forever.

John McPartlin

UNTITLED

Zeus smiles with wry humour,
Shaking his head,
These younger generations,
The muse of comedy, Thalia,
Shrieks with laughter,
At Mars, her brother God,
And his embarrassment,
Three crippled souls of twisted men,
Sacrilege, Insult and Humiliation,
Offered to his name,
Mercury tells all, to all,
Who will listen,
Aphrodite offers consolation,
In Her eyes, Mars sees,
The glint of humour,
And runs from her in shame,
In anger for the sacrifice,
He plans payment,
Lid loose,
Pandora's box lies on its side,
Clotho and Lachesis are spinning and weaving,
Atropos sits waiting with scissors ready,
From Vulcan a suit of armour ordered,
Well stroked the workshop's fires,
In Vesuvius,
Heap ashes on Pompeii,
Pride restored Mars laughs,
In the Underworld Pluto is stacking them in,
'Oops!' says Mars laughing,
'I meant just the Oracle.'
Gods, who'd be without one?

Hamish Lee

THE SUMMER PARADE

Warm summer sunlight shone above you from a blue summer sky,
as the warmth of the rays wrapped your chilled body in a comforting
                                                            blanket.

Strands of fine, blonde hair,
like newly spun silk threads, peep awkwardly from beneath your
                                                    blue sun hat
While days before, the rest of your crowning glory was shed to the
                                            mercy of the treatment.
Strewn like stubble in the wind.

Your blue eyes bulged and stared before you.
In desperation you hungrily drank the morphine from a brown
                                            glass bottle,
like any addict getting their fix.

The daily dosage went unheeded but not the pain.

Suddenly you smiled and raised your hand,
waving at the parade of chemically induced clowns as they passed
                                            you by.

The scene you described to me was in perfect detail,
but the show belonged only to you.

Clowns with pink permed fuzzy heads, rosy cheeks, orange noses
                                    and everlasting smiles,
all laughing silently as they somersaulted in your honour.
Music and laughter filled your ears alone,
as bubbles which never burst, floated carefree in this magical setting.

Now you lie sleeping,
worn and weak from the afternoon's activities.

The parade is over and the clowns have disappeared back into the
                                    brown, glass bottle,
ready to perform again tomorrow, pain permitting.

Sheila Chappell

WEE HARD NUT

You sit by the fire to read a good book
while Mum in the kitchen the dinner to cook
your father sits down to see what's on telly
while you look around for your one red welly.

You find it at last and go out to play
while Father watches telly with little to say
you go in the garden and run round about
while Mum puts out dinner gives you a shout.

So you sit down to dinner Mum, Dad and you
while big sister Annie is up in the loo
when Annie is called she's down quite smart
so now at last you can all make a start.

After your dinner it's back out to play
while Annie washes up Mum puts them away
you play in the garden till it's getting dark
then Mum calls you in to end all that.

You then get washed and ready for bed
while Mum looks around for your little Ted
he's your little bear so tender and sweet
the one you must have before you can sleep.

J Marshall

PADDY AND DOROTHY HARRINGTON

The Harbour soaks up a cooling, summer sun,
Where they walk together,
In their afternoon of life,
Holding hands and laughing,
The Music man and wife.
Travelling far to see new places, having fun,
May their twilight years be forever,
Always free from strife,
Irish eyes friendly, smiling,
The Music man and wife.
Mem'ries that will last with them forever,
Champagne toasted in that cooling summer sun,
Holding hands and laughing,
The Music man and wife.

J S Liberkowski

MAJESTIC, CRAGGY, MOUNTAINS

Majestic, craggy mountains, dressed in purple heather,
eagles soaring ever higher in the fine, spring weather.
Lambs are gambolling, running, jumping, having so much fun,
the shepherd tends his flock, such a busy season has begun.
Banks of bonny primroses gaily nod their heads as trains go by,
carrying happy holidaymakers towards the Isle of Skye.

Lochs strung around the country like a necklace,
sparkling sapphires and amethysts show no finer face.
Surrounded by grass as green as any emeralds rare,
such a beautiful land it's grace and beauty so fair.
It has a touching poignancy, when mists swirl all around,
centuries of history beckon as so many sightseers have found.

Tiny hamlets, lonely crofters cottages, provide solitude sublime,
giving a taste to busy folks visiting, a chance to step outside of time.
Busy towns and cities offer fun and shops galore;
even more history abounds for visitors to explore.
In every glen delights are found, all that nature can provide,
so many hearts have found a home in which they can reside.

The tossing of the caber, the hunting of the deer,
each pastime draws its own followers year upon year.
Haggis, porridge, shortbread too,
so many national dishes, these are but a few.
Of course - for fame - its nectar, which has an amber hue,
enjoys renown across the world, whiskies - there are a few!

The tartan and the sporran, the plaintive skirl of the pipes,
the highland fling, the reel and other dances of so many types.
Scotland's sons and daughters, through the ages, history have made,
as varied as a thistle, or a fawn hiding in a glade.
God made so much variety, within this lovely land,
so when you visit - stop - and see the creation of His hand.

Margi Hughes

WINTER WAXWINGS

Five Waxwings land on nearby branches bare,
Their crested heads distinctive in the trees.
They flit for days from tree to hedge to ground,
Gregarious, rare visitors are these.
Their red waxed-wings and yellow markings shine
While sunshine yellow tail tips light the sky,
The garden welcomes them in plumage bright
As through its shrubs and trees they feed and fly.
They eat their share of red viburnum berries
With beaks crammed full, they gorge this winter's feast.
Cotoneaster berries are devoured
Until the garden's food supply has ceased.
Waxwings innately know it's time to go,
So fly away, before it starts to snow.

Katrina Shepherd

MURPHY

He's bold and handsome, a big, brave, dark bay,
He'd refuse me nothing - he'll go all day.
His walk, trot and canter go on and on
He will try for me till his strength's all gone.
He made friends with my Old Boys from the start,
They're all quite upset when they're kept apart.
If left alone after all his labours
His *very* loud neighs disturb the neighbours.
I've met no other horse so sweet and kind,
Such a generous spirit's hard to find
A stable door ritual I wouldn't miss
Is his Polo, cuddle and goodnight kiss.

Judith A Jenkinson

ODE TO SCOTLAND

O'er the highland hills
Gaily clad in snow.
The music of majestic winds
So soft and gently blow.
O, listen to the moor fowl's call
From out the mists below.

I pause a while by a winding stream,
Close my eyes and dream
Of battles fought so long ago;
Of famous kings and queens
Who rule no more and of the ghosts
Of ships that carried them from
Many a distant shore.

The beauty of the lochs where
The water ripples frown
Capturing the shadows of the
Thistle's purple crown.
The crofters creels filled
With eels dot the silver
Shore. What joy, the skylark
Sings, and up into the darkest
Clouds does soar.

The sunset in the glens is a
Jewel to behold.
The long shadows of the trees
Bathed in blue and gold.
Medallions of white heather
Carpeting the land.
Scotland is an artist's dream
Touched by God's right hand.

Mary Angela Lisowska

THE GIFT OF LOVE

The world I'd give you gladly,
If it were mine to give.
And riches I'd bestow on you,
As long as I should live.

The sun I'd give you every day,
And stars to shine at night.
I'd take away your burdens,
And make life's journey light.

I'd give to you the peace of mind,
And wealth beyond belief.
No sadness would you have to bear,
Or suffer times of grief.

I'd like to take a life of bliss,
And place it in your hand.
But I can only give to you,
The gift of a humble man.

E P Burns

THE ROAD PAST MY DOOR

I've always lived on mainland.
It suits me very well:
the sense of freedom,
of being unshackled and unrestrained
apart from life's obligations and duties.
I heave great sighs of relief
as I realise that the road,
which passes my door,
leads anywhere I want it to.

I've seen to the scattered isles of the west.
I felt uneasy:
hemmed in, like a captive.
There, the road passing my door
led only to a ferry port.
I was at the mercy of pious believers,
held hostage by the dogma of holy men
and the whim of ferry companies -
'No Sunday sailings. Never will be'!

On weekdays, fervent doctrine relented.
Autocratic business bestowed blessing.
Then, nature intervened and ensured that
the road past my door led nowhere.
'All sailings cancelled due to stormy conditions'
'Prisoner! Prisoner'! My mind screamed.
On mainland, when the elements intervene,
I can go elsewhere than my chosen destination.
On western isle, only curtailment and stagnation.

Keith Lobban

A Brave Heart Song

I love the land wherein I was born
I love to see, not only, her green fertile tree
But the heather hills to walk among, so wild, wide and free
I love to hold, those said traditions of old
And hold boldly on to, to a higher degree
Scotland! My land, whereon now I stand
Is the only place, I want to be
Scotland my home, where once saints did roam
Where the brave covenanters, made martyrs
from their home, had to flee
Oh land of the Celt, of the tongue that's still felt
To be the mother tongue even to me
Brave hearts and true, ever were you
The land God had blessed, with a beauty so
True, wild and free.
To brave hearts I sing, may God help it wing
To see the end of deaths sting then praise be
As those covenanters of old, may we too be as bold
To take Scotland the message, of Christ's
Holy salvation, as we are told, to but do.

Margaret Lightbody

SCOTLAND

I've travelled far, but now I've come home
I climb up the hill to be alone,
I look at the scenery down below,
What in the world ever made me go, I just don't know
I love this place, I really do
Scotland is a beautiful place,
The scenery is out of this world,
The hills and glens, a pleasure to see,
All of this belongs to me.
I was born of this land, I'm proud you know
Of this land I love so,
My heritage, my traditions
To see the Scots man wearing the kilt,
It really gives your heart a lilt,
To hear the bagpipes play,
The Highland Games, a special day, mass bands
Swinging on their way,
The dancers in their tartan bright,
Dancing their hearts out all day.
The men tossing the caber, with all their might
It's all a beautiful sight.
I now know why, no matter where you go
The memories of Scotland you can't let go
It's your home, you are proud
Proud of this land you love so,
Scotland my home, how I love you.

Evelyn Adam

WISTFUL WINDFALL

Full in the crispness of the autumn air
I gather windfalls by the orchard trees
Like scattered jewels spilling bright and careless
From the treasure chests of brigand seas.
And breathing in the fragrance of the ripe -
Fleshed fruit; smooth, finger-firm; plump in their prime,
Musing, I gather memories that haunt
Like wistful windfalls from another time.
You were the apple on the topmost bough;
The choicest fruit that I was wont to claim,
But fecklessly I faltered, waiting for
The apple harvest breeze that never came.
Though autumn shades to winter on my brow
I sigh for apple breezes even now.

Walter Blacklaw

SILICON SPHERES

I want to write of ageless things,
Of rocks and roots and fairy glens
That hide amongst themselves a place
Of secret longing for the past.
A past when we were part of life
On earth; a crystal sphere
Infinitesimal . . .
A glint of light divine,
Unsullied by the greed of man
Hallowed in our lowly place
Amongst the trees and rocks and thorns.

We pass by:-
We stand but a little while
In mortal guise
Before returning to our ageless place
Amongst the grainy, sandy shore
Within the wave, the rock, the hollow
Wherein we find our resting place,
Until such time as beckons us
Away again, to face the world
Of greed and anger, hate and pain
With just a glint of light divine.

Teresa Maxwell

SCOTLAND'S MERMAID

At sixteen she saw the white lilies of Francoise
Later the rouge lion of Ecoze.
The fleur that blossomed,
To become; Maria Queen of the Scots.
Short her sometimes lonely life
West Lothian born 1543,
From Fotheringhay 43 years did she see.
Catherine de Medicio in her book of hours,
Tells how Frances loved Maria . . .
The Daughter of France returned,
To live her life of fear . . .
Her coins recall Henricus Darnley preceded her name . . .
The posters proclaimed; that Mary the fair;
Now the mermaid; must shoulder the blame.

Jean Daisy Herbert-Bradley

THE SPIRIT OF THE SCOTS

The spirit of the Scots is renowned
And all around Caledonia is to be found
And to befriend a true Scot is very good form
For they are forthright, helpful but with a yearning to roam
Very hardworking, dour, resolute, yet unusually polite
But to doubt their integrity would be taken as a slight
With a long historical heritage to cherish and preserve
A tradition that Bruce, Bonnie Prince Charlie and Wallace did serve
And as a proud nation, they fly their saltire with pride
For this is a country I would be proud to fight alongside
They sing of bloody battles and the flowering thistle
And how the skirl of the pipes must have made those redcoats bristle
They throw the hammer, toss the caber, and play curling
With the same strong spirit that won through, just south of Stirling
They built famous ocean-going liners on the industrial Clyde
And stood with just pride as down river they did glide.
Other smaller, but sturdy craft their fishing nets do ply
To stock the shops with a fresh and varied fish supply
Tough men battle with the elements to drill for gas and oil
And keep transport and industry going with their blood, sweat and toil
Well educated, with a wealth of poets, writers and inventors
Surely a source of much satisfaction to their mentors
With the likes of Burns, Baird, Fleming, Lister and Scott
No wonder the Scots say 'What a lot we've got'
Well known for colourful dancing and accordion musical sounds
Tourism, whisky, salmon fishing and woollen mills bring
                              in the pounds
Now many boring folk come on big blue coaches just to be seen
But most of these do not appreciate the true Scottish scene
They dislike the Scots, the pipes, and shun the haggis, tatties and neeps
And as they pass through fine scenery, read papers or fall into
                              deep sleeps.

Joseph Williams

NORTH OF THE BORDER

Every time I look at my map,
There she sits,
At the top of our tree,
A whole nation of people and places,
That are as foreign as Outer Mongolia to me,

I went there once when a bairn was I,
Apparently it rained and blew,
Snow-covered mountain and glen,
Fog and mist ensured the towns were lost,
We gave up and never went back again,

I ought to revisit,
Just to see what I missed,
Taking in the sights,
Perhaps a short stay,
Just one or two nights,

But I'm not stuck on,
Tossing the caber of eating haggis,
Or heather or thistle or tartan kilts or the pipers lament,
The Edinburgh Festival would be fine, perhaps I could get a tattoo,
Or spend my time in the hospitality tent,

I can truly say,
That from Scotland,
The only thing I really admire,
Is their anthem, The Flower of Scotland,
Which for some obscure reason fills me with passion and fire,

Being bonny or brave,
Have impressed me not,
Nor has Bonnie Prince Charlie, or Telford, Bell or Burns,
So to my roots way down south,
My mind and thoughts quickly returns.

P J Littlefield

WHEN IT'S . . .

When it's sunny I see you smile,
When it's raining I see you cry,
When it's cloudy I see you sad,
When it's windy I feel your warmth.
When it's night I see you wishing,
Wishing upon a star.
When it's dark I see you sleeping,
Sleeping so deep I see your dreams.
In your dreams I appear
Taking all your sorry thoughts away.
When it's dawn you awaken
With a smile across your face,
You're thinking of me, how do I know?
Because my soul lives within your heart.

Megan McKeracher

ON BEING FIFTY: ANOTHER VIEWPOINT

Old Age has hit me unawares -
Teeth? Hair? Oh yes, they're spares.

Ambitions sought, but never found,
Soon I'll be below the ground.

No figure any more,
Putting on clothes is just a chore.

Fighting flab that's bad for the heart,
The evil weed and I just cannot part.

Men? I've had a few too many -
And none of them left me a penny!

Children never came my way,
Well that's a price I had to pay.

A visit to the quack took away fertility,
I wish I could have ducked sterility.

Another cruise?
I must enthuse.

We wrinklies, we must stick together.
You know what they say about birds of a feather.

No friends; little money - all alone,
Well, for early sins I must atone.

Getting ready to dress up in my shroud.
Mustn't voice my fears too loud.

Old age, Death I fear, but most of all -
Osteoporosis hath me in his thrall.

F Cameron

SCOTTISH FORTS

A landscape of beauty its scenery filled
With fragrant, wild heather growing upon the hills
Magnificent mountains, high towering spires
Monarchs and poets were wholly inspired.

The tartan plaids of ancestral clans
Where history dates back to the ancient land
Fierce battles took place and were bravely fought
And the proudly Scots protected their forts.

Rebecca Humphries

ANGUINE HIPS

With sanguine lips
And anguine hips,
She glides across the hall.
A dozen dancers in her wake
Two dozen in her thrall.
With subtle gropes
And gracious ease
She raises hopes,
A tactile tease,
Then slips into a stranger's chair
And almost out of almost bare.
A would-be lover without name
Has bought a bottle of champagne
And poured it, chilled, into her glass
As she had poured and filled her dress.
And as the bubbles dance her tongue
She flows onto the floor again.
And dances on
Till three or four -
Staff agitate towards the door.
But when the rest
Have gone to bed,
She'll dance the DJ
In her head.

Jonathan Swann

SPRING HAS SPRUNG

The winter days were long,
I was feeling really low,
I longed for warmer air,
And the sun to make me glow.

Then suddenly it came,
Like a spirit in the night,
Spring had sprung its magic,
And now my world looked bright.

Looking from my garden,
I saw a cloudless sky,
The sun warmed my body,
I waved my blues goodbye.

A blackbird on the apple tree,
Announced it with his song,
And all around I found the clues,
That proved he wasn't wrong.

There was a bud, a shoot, a flower,
All anxious to appear,
I was so overcome,
I shed a little tear.

And so I stood in reverence,
I said a little prayer,
And thanked God my Creator,
For the beauty everywhere.

M Findlay

FOCHABERS SQUARE 2000

Like a' big projects, there's against and there's for
A millennium feat for fowk t' adore
Set oot as a heritage, oor young t' implore
In th' annals o' history o' Fochabers folklore.

The whole episode has caused a lot o' het air
By th' residents discussin' this important affair
It just goes t' show, there are people who care
An' who wint t' mak' sure, we've an attractive square.

The lavvies had t' go, th' bus shelter tee
T' mak' room for some slabs an' a seat
Ten auld lime trees hid t' come doon an' a'
T' be replaced by maples more neat.

Committees were formed an' meetin's held
An' a th' het air caused a breeze
Which blew through th' centre o' Fochabers
An' nearly ca'ad ower th' auld trees.

The maple replacements are noo growin' fine
Some skwint wi' a tilt t' th' north
After a' th' het air dis onybody care
Aboot th' trees or fit they were worth.

A few hardy annuals look aifter th' trees
They were there durin' days an' at nights
Stuck up in the air in a cherry picker chair
To fix a bonnie array o' wee lichts.

Consensus o' opinion o' th' Fochabers fowk
Is th' trees are lookin' richt braw
Wi' th' lichts intertwined, ye'll go a lang wye t' find
A bonnier pickter t' draw.

Robbie Innes

AN EVENT

Has Christmas become just an event
To be celebrated but once a year?
A time for gifts and gatherings
Of kindness and good cheer
Have we forgotten to remember
It's about the birth of Christ?
Our God becoming human
And sharing in our life.

Has Easter become just an event
To be celebrated in the spring?
A time of eggs and daffodils
Of palms and hymns to sing
Have we forgotten to remember
It's about the death of our Christ?
Followed by resurrection
And the promise of new life.

Has Communion become just an event
To be celebrated now and then?
A piece of bread, a cup of wine
Small thanks and muttered amen
Have we forgotten to remember
It's the body and blood of Christ?
A symbol in our church
A monument in our life.

Has church become just an event
To be attended on a Sunday?
With Jesus lifted high
Then ignored again on Monday
Have we forgotten to remember
It's all about our Christ?
To walk with Him continually
In the centre of our life.

Ron Beaton

CULLODEN

Upon a desolate, bleak moor,
Lie tears and blood, grief and lament,
Too many to cry for,
Too few to weep for the dead,
Too many corpses to bury,
Too few to bury them,
Only shrouded death to count their numbers,
Only death to cackle at her work,
Fate that day had gone a riot,
Pillaged towns - flee to darkness,
Too few to seek refuge in craggy hills,
English dogs to march triumphant,
Let Scotland for eternity,
Ne'er forgive or forget,
The lamentable mark.

Alan Pow

A CRY FOR PEACE

Look upon this troubled world where reigns there so much strife,
See murders, violence, bombings as part of daily life.
It's just across a troubled sea some people want release,
But are their words from tear-filled eyes
Alas, a cry for peace.

Children born every day, are born into hope,
But we the ageing already know life's one big slippery slope.
Do men with guns never hear while piling on the grease?
The child's voice scream from far beyond
Alas, a cry for peace.

Religious creeds may vary through a variety of races,
But bullets, bomb blasts cannot see the innocence on faces.
They maim and injure one and all our hearts they weep, please cease,
As stricken families grieve their dead
Alas, a cry for peace.

Forget your lettered titles, please drop your hatred too,
Open your eyes and look around, they're just the same as you.
Look forward to the future, think of all around,
If you're too busy arguing, you'll never hear the sound
A cry for peace.

Jim Fraser

EARLY SPRING

Joyous are the songs
Of the birds that sing
Heralding the dawn
Of a newborn spring
Daffodils - tulips, crocus too
Show off their beauty
As they come on view.

Aided by the hilltops' melting snow
Rivers and streams swiftly flow
A little bud, a tiny thing
Tells us winter is nearly gone
It was all so beautiful for a while
But it is the spring
The early spring
To our hearts that brings a smile.

Peter P Gear

IT'S NO THE DAY!

Hae ye ever tried ti rhyme
when the rain is poorin doon
an aathing's black an grey an weet
an misery's aroond?
It's like that nou, just as a write;
ma umbarellie's yaseless;
a've hud tae walk through poorin rain -
a'm weet an coffee's tasteless.
A've nae agreed wi those a meet;
a'm cauld an baith ma feet are weet,
denied frae haein ma favourite seat -
an aa around a face defeat.
There's those wha rise above it aa
some by climbin up the wall
some by writing hoo they feel
an me, by lettin oot a squeal
o nae poetic quiet acceptance,
but nanetheless wi some reluctance
a tak ma pen for pure relief -
but end it aa - in disbelief!
It's no the day for writin rhyme -
jist hing aroond an pass the time;
the morn'll come - nae doot at aa,
an doon ye'll come frae up the waa!

Andrew A Duncan

Dark Angel

All you see is her pretty face,
The smiles and laughter,
The angel figure present before you.
You cannot break the surface water.
Beneath it all lies something dark,
Encased in light to protect the world.
It holds inside all thoughts of death,
Keeping away all means of pain,
The thunderbolt to bring you down.
But the struggle is on between light and dark.
Darkness closing in on her,
Tick-tock, tick-tock,
Snuffing the candles, putting them back in the box,
Tick-tock, tick-tock,
Got to stop that clock.
Cold hands gripping at her heart,
Slowly draining out life,
Releasing the darkness into the world.
A test of strength has begun,
The victor lies in life or death.
The angel's toying with your mind,
She's tearing you apart,
The darkness breaks her defences down,
It's tearing at her heart.
The love is somewhere still inside,
But can you find the flame in time,
To reignite her angel light?

Ruth Mackie

BLUE

Grey, oh so grey
But beyond
Beyond that horizon
There was such beauty
Such wealth
Will I ever know
If I can but trust in what I should
That reward will come
I know
I know it will
Across that horizon
Now, oh so blue and golden
I have found what I could have lost
When I did not trust when I could.

A Macleod

HURTING

Part water, part rain, I'll never regain my true love
From an ocean of tears, am drowning with sorrow and emptiness
Hoping I can swim from this broken heart,
My spirit is low, not knowing where to go,
Tigers claw at my head, wishing now I was dead,
Doves weep over by, dropping flowers from the sky,
Petals rain inside my soul soothing my everlasting pain,
Red carnations - I give to you, out of love,
Heaven take my body lay it down on love rain,
Let it flow towards my lady in Venus,
To her blue fire that I desire, orbit me from my hurt,
Just one time, with some red wine,
When you're around me I dance on satin, smooth as silk,
Kicking gold-dust over the moon,
Please give me a chance or even one glance
As you ride by on your mystical silver cloud,
Stars gaze my eyes blinding me from you,
I feel your hair caress my face,
But I can't see you in all your grace,
My mind's going crazy full of Astra cars
Racing to get out of this love from above,
Wishing upon a star, you take me for who I am -
Your silent loving man.

H Muir

SCATTERED BUT FRUITFUL OF PURPOSE

Who knows through truth and trust
With document proof and signs of rust
Those roots in land and name
The source of character inclination fame
That allegiance sign of belonging to some nation kind.

Whose cause and gift of inspiration
Set the tone and speed of its creation

On how to wither, rise and fall
With sense of longing of roots origin restore
Yet seeks a nation for all world own care

Gordon Walters

SUMMER'S ENCHANTMENT

The skies all grey, there's a nip in the air
birds have deserted, the trees are bare
but the rhythm of nature as it edges along
gives us time for reflection now summer has gone
nature's intricate finery has said farewell
her colours resplendent o'er hill and dale.
Purple heather braes, meadows fresh and green
graceful swans on silver water glides serene
sheep dotted on hillsides, contented cows lazing
fields white with daisies, ponies grazing
good husbandry of farmers grace country roads,
ripe plump berries, fat peas in their pods,
banks of white clover scented, lush and deep,
Warm evening breath, sunset shadows creep,
the great transformer slowly sinks to rest,
Magical splendour lingering in the west.
A wealth of golden memories, a season now lost.
One morning soon we may expect frost.

Greta Craigie

THE SNOWDROPS

The snowdrops shone like crystals,
alive in the morning sun,
leaves and petals drooped with dew;
a new day had begun.

Spiders' webs like silken threads,
glistened in the mist,
and every flower in the lea,
Mother Nature kissed.

Shades of pink and lilac,
unfold up in the sky,
and if you listen closely,
you can hear the meadow sigh.

As the sun shone brightly,
pure rays of golden light,
a golden eagle spreads its wings,
a most glorious sight in flight.

A MacGregor

STENCH

Sunday was like a desert
 as we drove in to the country
  barren fields as far as the eye could see
  empty of life, terrifying me
  an eerie sense of foreboding
   rising like a mist
   and there on the horizon
    smoking white and ghostly
     the vapour of a bovine pyre
     mysteriously lit, and
     as we drove closer
      smoke became denser
       cattle on a railway sleeper
       like an overturned table
       legs rigid heavenward
        as I asked God for forgiveness
         that a healing rain would quench
         that sadness and the hopelessness
         and the aromatic stench

of farmers' tears going down the drain
 to a land called rack and ruin
 this holocaust remove it Lord
 I still feel there's trouble brewing
  disaster is imminent, unless we change our ways
  the countryside stutters agriculture
  and on every fence and stump
   the heart the blood that pumps
    is dressed just like a nemesis called vulture

David Isaac

STILLNESS

As the mist caresses the surface of the still loch -
Its fingers comb the firs on the enfolding hills.
A lone heron watches, in silence, from a protruding rock
And the world is at peace as nature and weather work their wills.

The snow still lingers, clothing all in virgin white.
Icicles, like the droplets of a chandelier, hang down.
The landscape becoming an ethereal, dream-like sight,
As if dressed for a ball in a glistening, shimmery gown.

Above, in the heavens, not a cloud besmirches the blue of the sky,
Not a breath of wind disturbs the stillness of the trees.
The watery sun shines down, as if it would like to cry
At the beauty God gave us in scenes such as these.

Nettie Killen

VANISHING POINT

Picture The Mystery and Melancholy of a Street of 1914.
The horsebox is flung open; there's a nightmare in the back.
Like the Marie Celeste - what does it all mean?
Tramlines veer off canvas - away off track.
Is it from a reverie - a hallucination - or a real scene?
Beware the shadows - plague black.
Strange girl with rolling hoop - you flit across the street.
Who is the shadowy figure you're dying to meet?

Beware the fifteen arches with the black arrow.
Where's the birds' song in this sinister place?
Watch the horizon of cadmium yellow.
Have the inhabitants disappeared without a trace?
I lose myself in Chirico's street, although a creepy place to go
- With black-eyed windows staring into space;
And a red flag saluting the blue-green air
- As mystery fills this painted square.

Here's a back-drop to a surreal play.
Those tramlines symbolise the railway engineer - Giorgio's father.
It's always dusk in this Italian day.
Papa bullied Giorgio and his younger brother.
As a child he was often sickly.
The arcade's arches symbolise the artist's mother.
Chirico argued this masterpiece wasn't his work.
Now this strange, sad street hangs in New York.

Mark Young

THE PASSING OF PETER

He gazed into my eyes as I held him cuddled in,
And to tell of his love for me, he licked my bristly chin.
I think he knew deep in his heart he wasn't here forever,
The sands of time were running out, he'd reached the end of tether!

I had him as a tiny pup, some fourteen years ago,
When life was full of things to do (except when I said 'No').
He didn't think that he'd get old . . . well, as if he would!
But he completed our small family as only Peter could!

Now he's old and battle-scarred . . . all grey around the muzzle.
His joints are all arthritic, his hold on life a puzzle.
His eyes are filming over and he blindly bumps around,
His ears strain to listen to each decreasing sound!

I knew that he was suffering even though he couldn't talk.
I couldn't make him better though I watched him like a hawk.
It was 'make your mind up' time for me . . . how awkward could it get?
I *knew* the only answer was to take him to the vet!

It was with awf'ly heavy heart that I carried him to town,
And only when I reached the vet could I bear to put him down.
The vet was really kind to me . . . of course, he understood.
He did his best to cheer me up, but it wasn't any good!

I asked him if he'd suffer from the needle he'd inject,
And what would happen to him as the contents took effect.
'He'll just go off to sleep like he has done every night,
Except that he won't wake up again to pain and loss of sight!'

I miss my mate, old Peter . . . the kids all miss him too.
The house seems awf'ly empty . . . no dog with bone to chew.
His collar and his lead hang forlornly from their hook
Awaiting his successor when I've got the heart to look!

G K (Bill) Baker

THE ENCOURAGER

One who stands
Beside you if you fall
And helps you crawl
To safety.
Who does not shout
Or cry out, but rather
Envelopes your needs
In deeds of love.
Who walks with you
Through the dark night
In spite of the jeering
Of the leering crowd.
Who supports your feet
In sweet steps
Of silence . . .
Who speaks with soft tones
To the very bones
Of your nature.
Who never pours water
To slaughter your fire
Of bright flames.
Who is always there
To share your hopes
And dreams and plans and schemes.
One who understands, and only
Hands you truth,
And one who loves you so well
In the swelling tides of pain and gain
And in all your sprains of life
And death.

Judith Thomas

Nature's Cleaning Days

Wind wipes the weather-vane and sweeps
The cockerel from his perch,
Then with each puff proceeds to buff
The tarnished silver birch.

When besom branches beat the air,
The brittle twigs go 'snap'.
Boughs lean and spare say, 'It's not fair.
We're running out of sap!'

A helpful gust removes all dust,
Then tells his squirrel friend
To take a broom to brush his room
Now winter's soon to end.

Rain rubs and scrubs the laurel shrubs
And clears away all trace
Of dirt and grime, so in due time
It leaves a spotless place.

Frost gives a sheen, adds lustre keen
To polish stiffened grass.
It makes each blade look custom made
Like elfin swords of glass.

Now flakes of snow bring brighter glow
To winter's laundry scene,
Washing the land with sudsy hand
So everything looks clean.

Celia G Thomas

I KNOW GOD FORGIVES

I'm nursing now a broken heart; from all my loved ones torn apart,
My happiness seems far away, the price of sin I have to pay.
There's nothing left of what I had, the pain of this makes me so sad.
But I know there's someone up above, it's my Heavenly Father full
                                                    of love
He daily watches over me and deals with me so tenderly.
He's ever-ready to forgive; He'll heal my hurt and let me live
A life of service in His care, I'm sorry now so I'll be there.
Just listening for His loving voice, I thank Him that I have the choice
To carry on, or turn around, and follow Him for then I've found
A broken heart, He soon will mend, when time with Him we
                                                    freely spend
The blood of Jesus cleanses me, from all my sin and sets me free.

Alison Czajkowski

AT THE BEACH

The sea ripples,
Like flames across gasoline.
Burning the feet of the bathers,
Stumbling in the chilled water,
Like scorched stuntmen in,
Cheap action movies.
Must be horror flicks I think.
Watching the living dead,
Veer along the shoreline.
Every step is their last,
Sunburnt flesh and shawls.
I smile,
As the woman in the red shirt,
Laughs at her shaven husband's,
Broken shades.

M Howard

PRECIOUS MEMORIES

There is a path of precious memories
From here to Heaven above
That keeps us close together
It's called the path of love
And down the path of memories
We gently tread each day
And our thoughts are with you
As life goes on its way
You left us precious memories Dad
That makes us laugh and cry
But the love you planted in our hearts
No millionaire could buy
Sad are the tears that fall
Living our lives without you
Is the hardest part of all.

Wendy Lynne Bryan

REMEMBERING YOU

In the early morning mist,
With the white of the clouds above.
In the evening sky and setting sun,
The green of the trees,
And the brown of the mighty Earth.
In the glorious rainbow after the shower,
I will remember you.

Lingering perfume from the flowers,
With the song of the bird from above.
And the roar of the wind,
The breaking waves and pounding sea.
As they crash against the rocks
And the rustle of the corn.
As it grows in the fields
I will remember you.

In the grass under my feet,
And the breeze in my hair.
The falling rain and wind blowing in my face.
In the steady beat of an untiring heart,
And in the depth of my being,
I will remember you.

Elisabeth Dill Perrin

THE BOX

Amongst the boxes in the attic
One stands out alone
Covered in dusty old paper
Containing a single bone.

No-one knows who put it there
Or where the box came from
But everyone avoids the attic
When the light from the window is gone.

Once, long ago, so the story goes
A young boy was home alone
Deciding to search the attic
He soon discovered the bone.

From that day on, his senses were gone
And no-one knew how or why
But deep asleep in the middle of the night
'It was the bone!' he'd cry.

Rumours spreading as they do
Some thought the bone *possessed*
And only the very brave
Would look: hazarding a guess.

From everywhere people came
To solve the riddle of the bone.
Until an old man arrived
Insisting he examine it: Alone!

Later the bone was found in a box
Wrapped with paper and with twine
Beside it, on a note was written
'Leave! The bone is mine!

No-one knows who put it there
Or where the bone was from.
But everyone avoids the attic
When the light from the window is gone!

Maureen Thomas

ILLUSIONS

I cannot waste
my breath
on you
any longer . . .
I guess this
means
that I no longer
love you;
as I stare at the face
in the mirror
beside my bed,
and wonder if
I ever did,
or was it an
illusion,
my mind
masked
as it so often
is . . .
I'll try not
to make
the same mistake
again . . .

Jade Watkins

MEDITATION

We are born to live our lives
The way we feel is best
God gave us talents to perfect
Not sit at home and rest.

We have a chance to prove ourselves
To do as we would choose
To show our gifts and use our brains
To win and not to lose.

Fame will not come to us
If we sit back and fret
We must go forward with confidence
And be more fearless yet.

But what if fate should come our way
And we should fail to do
All the things we thought we could
Dreams not yet come true.

So we must take a grip on life
Not let it smother us
And day by day we should improve
If we love and trust.

Robert Lewis

WHAT NATURE CAN BRING

As I walk along the hillside
A soft breeze passes by gently
Surrounded by the sweet smell of nature
I slowly close my eyes
Even though my eyes see darkness
My mind creates a scene
I can hear the sound of wildlife
With a soft, gentle hum of bees
I imagine a field full of daisies
At the centre, stands a small tree
The birds have covered the branches
They all sing a soft melody
The sound of their songs makes me sleepy
So I lay in the daisies so calm
I gaze at the sky with a smile on my face
The petals, they tickle my palms
I think about life and its reasons
I wonder, why are we here?
We're surrounded by a world full of beauty
Yet, some people don't even care
I'm proud to live in the valleys
Surrounded by nature alone
I'm proud to be able to smell the fresh air
I'm proud to call it my home.

Matthew Thomas Williams

PRECIOUS TIME

Once a woman's role in life
Was as a mother and a wife.
Her husband earned the daily bread
To keep her and their children fed.
But both parents work today,
'One wage is not enough,' they say,
'For mortgage, holidays and toys,
Computers for our girls and boys.'
There are times when they can't be there
When their children need their care.
Grandparents help to fill the breach
If they don't live out of reach,
But they have seen their children grown
They may want lives of their own,
Or there may be none around
Then childminders must be found
And the fees that parents pay
Melt the second wage away.
Apart from that, children would rather
Have their mother or their father
Home, each day, with time to spend
With them, when school comes to an end.
Computers and holidays are fine
But the best gift for a child is time.

Pamela Evans

THE BLUEBELL WOOD

O perfect beauty of this lovely wood
Where bluebells gently sway beneath the trees
And through the fresh green leaves the sun sends shafts
Of golden glory shimmering in the breeze.
But suddenly the lark's supernal song
Stills the pure air and captivates the mind,
The soul is lifted to a higher sphere
A brief sweet taste of paradise to find.
One moment, and the heavenly glimpse is gone,
The foretaste of eternity was good!
God's gracious presence lingers in this place
Filling with peace and joy the Antrim wood.

Pearl Reynolds

WALKING ON SNOW

Walking on freshly
fallen snowflakes
layers of delicate
petals fragment
beneath my feet,
the delicacy of
nature as fragile
as relationships
crumbling in the
wee small hours
of another night.

Mary Guckian

THE SQUIRREL AND ME

'I'm having a nut for my tea,'
said the bushy-tailed squirrel to me.
'My body is strong
with a tail ever so long
and I live my life up in a tree.
Its trunk I use for some fun,
playing peek-a-boo, then I will run
hoping you will keep watching me
and my babies' drey you won't see.'

Maureen Dawson

Times Have Changed

If Great, Great Grandma did return
She would open wide her eyes
When she saw the mod cons of our day
She would get a big surprise.

To see cosy homes electrified
Carpets and our central heat
And watch the world news on TV
Would surely be a treat.

And then, at the press of a button
Dishes and clothes are washed clean
The microwave, fridge and the freezer
Are things which she'd never seen.

Down town she would meet a lady
With her mobile phone in hand
Or watch the people from 'the wall'
Get banknotes on demand!

We would tell her of keyhole surgery
Of laser treatment for the eye.
Of the man who had his arm sewn on
'Unbelievable' would be her reply.

And then we could take her to visit
Her friends across the seas
It would only take hours and minutes
While she sat there at her ease.

To see all these modern inventions
To her, or so it would seem
That these were just things of fantasy
And this was only a dream.

Nell Thompson

DUNOON'S AIN FAIRY QUEEN

One day, long, long ago, I wis up at my Grannie Cairns'
Me wee Auntie Sarah wis telt tae 'Look after that bairn!'
She sat me oan her lap, an' pointing tae wan o' the tiles
O ma Grannie's parlour fireplace (it wis typical o' Argyll an'
                                        the Isles)
Says she, 'Look here at this bonnie, bonnie rose!
Who dae ye think lives there, dae ye suppose?
Nane other than the Queen of a' the fairies,
With her royal maids o' honour - Beatrice and Mary!'
Then - the greatest secret she confided -
(She'd share it wi' me - she decided!)
She wis in fact the Fairy Queen!
I wis that excited - I almost screamed!
But ma favourite wee Auntie put her finger tae her lips!
'Wheesht noo Paddy hen! This is *oor secret!* Dinna let it slip!

When moonlight did brighten the night sky
Magic dust wis sprinkled on her frae on high -
And she'd change frae ma cuddly wee Auntie Sarah,
Tae the maist beautiful Fairy Queen! There wis none fairer!

Many years have passed - how fast time runs -
I'm noo a grannie, Daniel 'n' Connor are ma wee grandsons.
But tae me, ma Fairy Queen is just the same
Though now she wears glasses, hair o' grey - a different surname!
Her consort called her his 'wee Sally,'
And I believe wi' Beatrice 'n' Mary she's still pally!

However, she is still my ain wee Fairy Queen
The jolliest, kindest wan you've ever seen!

I cannae wait until ma wee grandweans grow
Old enough fur me tae tell them that Grannie knows
Whaur the Fairy Queen does bide, in that bonnie, bonnie rose!
An' in the rosebuds reside wee fairies dancin' oan their tippy-toes!
It'll be *oor* secret. Naw, naw, we'll no tell -
That we ken whaur the fairies dwell!

Patricia Cairns Laird

VICTIMS

Sad gaunt faces, staring haunted eyes
No future beyond the next desperate fix
Despised by everyone, never seen as victims
Why should we care? They brought it on themselves.

If they were starving animals, would we turn away disgusted?
Would we be embarrassed or ignore their plight or pain?
Could we show more mercy or try to offer sympathy?
Comfort and understanding, show a little respect?

These tormented souls have lost their pride and dignity
Slaves to their habit, they have no self-control
A menace to society, these drug-ridden junkies
All belong to someone, it could be you or I.

Agnes Cowan

HEALING THOUGHT
(For Sylvia)

Gracious Spirit to you I pray
Please walk beside me throughout my day
On my life's journey, on this earth plane
For Your guidance I ask, time and again.

For your power to be with me in Thy healing room
Please be with me, pray make it soon
Your presence here, may it be strong
Your love sincere, as I feel Your warmth.

O Gracious Spirit as I pray to You
Thy healing work that I may do
Pray comfort me, as I go on my way
Carrying out Your work, day by day.

Please stay by me, please stay a while
Please make me happy, help me share a smile
Let us bond together, as we work and pray
In this, Your church, and throughout our day.

Pray send a thought, pray send Your love
Pray send from higher side above
O Gracious Spirit, divine and true
May I send a healing thought for You.

Graham Macnab

THE BIRDS IN WINTER

The overnight snow which has settled
on the dried heads of the sedums
looks for all the world like
giant powder puffs. It is
an enchanting landscape, pure, pristine.

The blackbird stands out, so dark
against the white-festooned branches,
until he flies out, scattering
the snow, in his vain attempt
to find food. The smaller birds,
stand miserably huddled, feathers
puffed up against the cold,
hopefully awaiting the few crumbs
cast out of the back door.

Gone are the days of quiet bonhomie,
pecking alongside one another.
Now each one guards his spoil,
attacking, molesting those others
who dare to come anywhere near.

Do they know, as we do,
that spring will soon be here?
That their daily larder
will be filled with 'natural' food?
Like us, they must revel
in the soft warmth of spring days,
quickly forgetting the harsh despair
of winter. Abundant food for their
growling families, flitting around our gardens,
and pouring out their joy and gratitude
in a long series of trilling song.

Joyce Hockley

OVER THE MOON

Life - it throws you sometimes
The direction who can say
But I'm glad that I have found myself
Over the moon today

Didn't need a spaceship
To get me off the ground
Just felt a lovely feeling
About everything around

I've longed to be here many times
And often made a start
The desire so deep within me
Seemed to always fall apart

So I'm sending invitations
A party - late in June
And if you're free, come join me
The venue - Over The Moon

Bring all your friends and family
You'll have lovely time
No need to get dressed up
Casual - that's just fine

And when the party's over
We've danced the night away
Earth beckons you to go back home
Don't - I want you all to stay

Mary Corsie

IN BETHLEHEM

The Babe was lying in a manger bare -
The Ass, the Oxen and the Sheep were there,
Gazing down with placid, star-bright eyes
'Neath old beams open to the velvet skies.

The Shepherds brought their humble gifts
And Kings their three-fold tributes there did bring;
As Joseph knelt and tended Mary's child
The Babe looked up, curled a fist and smiled.

So tenderly his gentle Mother sang;
The Oxen lowed - the very rafters rang
With joyous happiness, for Christ was born
In quiet Bethlehem, on Christmas morn.

Frances Reed

CHRISTMAS 2000

Wasn't it lovely to see the snow?
Falling so gently, soft and white.
Covering the dull grey earth below
Making it clean and pure and bright.

Streets and gardens covered in snow
Leafless branches adorned with white.
Nature making a Christmas show
Stars in the night sky sparkling bright.

How all the children loved the snow
Sledging down the hill in the park.
Throwing snowballs, their faces aglow
Playing out doors until it grew dark.

Wasn't it lovely to see it go?
Slipping off roofs and dripping off trees.
Thawing slowly, ever so slow
Everyone hoping it wouldn't freeze.

Wasn't it great to go out again?
And walk in the streets free of ice.
Chat to the neighbours, don't mind the rain,
Back to normal. Isn't it nice?

Netta Jess

SCHOOL

I wish there was no rule to say,
Children had to go to school,
I'd stay at home all day and play,
Then my day would be really cool.

School dinners are very disgusting,
Semolina and mushy peas,
The cook isn't always very trusting,
I wouldn't be surprised if you got a disease.

Maths and science are both so boring,
French is terrible too,
I'd rather be outside exploring,
Than learning the length of Peru.

'School can be very useful,'
So everyone has said,
But will teachers be very grateful,
When I get a degree in sleeping in bed.

Siobhan Anderson (11)

FAREWELL TO DAD

You saw us through nearly fifty years
Through all of our laughter and all of our tears
You were always a gentleman of the highest degree
And we'll live up to your advice to be all we can be

Our family strength has been our love for each other
A father, four kids and a wonderful mother
As we grew up we wanted to make you proud
And as a family unit we stood out in a crowd

Although we are scattered both near and far
No journey's too long with the aid of a car
We'll look after Mum as you'd want us to do
And strong in our thoughts will always be you

We've said our goodbyes and let you move on
But you're still in our hearts so you'll never be gone
We'll try not to cry or be overly sad
But suffice to say we'll really miss you Dad.

Edith MacDonald-Clark

A Gift From Scotland

The bard of Scotland, Robert Burns,
Well-known o'er land and sea,
As the years roll on and truth unfurls,
A prophet seems to be.
The writing of his poems and songs
For the people of *his* time
And the message given of rights and wrongs,
So strongly fit our 'clime'.

As we live the new millennium
With all *our* doubts and fears
And look at Rabbie's legacy
Across the many years,
We find that *he* was full of care
With worries large and small,
Sometimes the load too great to bear,
Encroaching like a pall.

Consumerism - conflict - greed,
Throughout the land were rife,
As farms gave way to industry.
Which became the way of life.
But Burns taught the lasting values -
Felt sure they'd 'bear the gree',
Putting faith in human nature
With its special dignity.

His forthtelling, not foretelling
Is what makes our bard a seer,
The commoner, the ordinary
No title needed here,
Can bring about, he stresses,
A fellowship of peace,
A time of joy and love,
When all the conflicts cease.

What better gift can Scotland bring
To a world bereft of sense
Than this urge to strive for harmony,
Relations never tense.
Burns is a poet for humankind
Of any creed and race,
As his wisdom and his hopefulness
Leap over time and space.

Edie Garvie

MISTY ISLES

When you hear the bagpipes
See the swirl of the kilts
You will know, over the border
In Scotland you are.
A land steep'd
In history and legend
Rugged landscapes
Intriguing lochs.
Mystery, yet to enfold
Abode of Robert Burns
A poet of great renown
And Alexander Bell, I hear tell.
The trossachs'
Magic glens will captivate you.
Stroll through the heather
'Neath mountains, so grand
As panoramic beauty
Unfolds over the land.
Scotland a jewel
Beyond compare
With hospitality they love to share.
So with the drone of the bagpipes
As you end your trek,
Haste-ye-back
Even be you, a sassenach.

Margaret Parnell

LAKESIDE MEDITATION

Yet him, whose heart is ill at ease,
Such peaceful solitudes displease,
He loves to drown his bosoms far
Amid the elemental war
And my black, Palmer's choice had been
Some ruder and more savage scene,
Like that which frowns round dark
Lock Ken,
There eagles scream from isle to shore;
Down all the rocks, the torrents roar;
O'er the black waves, incessant driven
Dark mist infect, the summer heaven;
Through the rude barriers of the lake;
Away its hurrying waters break.
Faster and whiter dash and curl,
Till down yon dark abyss they hurl,
Rises the fog-smoke white as snow,
Thunders the viewless stream below,
Diving as if condemn'd to love
Some demon's subterranean cave,
Who prison'd by enchanter's spell,
Shakes the dark rock with groan and yell
And well that Palmer's form and mien;
Had suited with the stormy scene,
Just on the edge, straining his ken.
To view the bottom of the den,
Where, deep, deep down and far within,
Toils with the rocks, the roaring lin;
Then, issuing forth one foamy wave
And wheeling round the giant's grave,
White as the snowy charger's tail;
Drives down the pass of
Kenadale.

M Titcombe

THE BUTTERFLY

When poppies grow among the grass
the gentle rain comes falling fast
the wind blows havoc with the trees
and the branches dance n the breeze
and plays a two-step for the blossoms and the bees.
A worm wriggles in the grass
he cannot move very fast
a bird flew down and picked him up
and dropped a feather for good luck.
The butterfly comes out to play
among the flowers he is so gay
over the swaying grass he swept,
over the flowers he soared and leapt.
He came to the garden to make love to the lily
but a wind got up and blew him silly
he landed in among the sticky-willy,
he kissed a rose instead of the lily.
Poor lily wept as she held hear head
and thought that her butterfly was dead.
This is how there is a droop at the lily
and a blush on the rose.

Helen Manson

SKYE

You are sunny, windy,
Bright and hazy,
Blue and misty,
My wingèd isle
My homeland.

Birch trees tossing,
White waves racing,
Wild clouds scudding,
The scent of thyme
The cobalt sea.

Jagged peaks of basalt,
Long dead volcanoes,
Ghosts in ruined houses,
Your past in your present
Sets me free.

Lorna Ferguson Kirk

THE LADY OF THE LODGE

She gave herself the title 'The Lady of the Lodge'
But no one would disagree with her
They said she had learning difficulties
Before she came to the Lodge to live
In truth we learned a lot from her and she had much to give
We were cautious
She showed us how to be spontaneous
We were reserved
While she was open hearted and loving
We contrived to relate
But she was totally true to herself at all time
Being so self assured she inadvertently exposed our self-consciousness
All this was crowned with a natural ability to laugh
And simply be happy
Such was the Lady of the Lodge
She was one of life's butterflies
We were privileged to hold her in our hands
To behold her beauty for a short time
Now we must open our hands and allow her to fly away.

W Campbell

I Am Already Less

It's just like the thing
When I get it together and sort it out
The weaving starts, the searching, the mingling
Covering my mind, then my soul
The sea of love closes in, an empty beach fills over
Slowly so I don't realise
Stealthily so I do not expect
Every day I'm sinking deeper - the shallow disappears.
She's captivating - not my eye, but my mind.
     I am already less when she's not there.

And then it's just like the thing
I already made a vow and have a purpose.
Why these feelings then? They seem unfair.
Is it not against the rules, against the design and anyway
Where does the interest lie - with her? With me?
There is no touch, no kiss, no lingering look
Only comfort in presence
Meetings in mind
I'm longing for the next day when the tide comes in
And her words pour over me.
     I am already less now she's not here.

Vivienne Bern

SUBURBIA - MY DREAM

Lurid and obscure . . .
My dream of houses
With scarce weeds in strips of gardens,
Low walls and concrete facades
But well designed
Facades of concrete and cement and dingy stone
Hiding soft-skinned families
In cheerful deprivation
Of terraces (or cosy holes).

And poverty written on the walls
In vivid carefree colour.
I walked through avenues of cartoons
And the suburbs stretches suburbia to these estates.

The children could play football in the streets
Laughing in their ill-fitting clothes
And laughing through the tight-skinned sallow flesh,
All would be catchable
In one nostalgic memory
Romanced and made for oils.

I remember coughing
And going back to the land of soft skins.
I remember . . .
As though a communist would feel repulsion
Touch me with apologetic beauty.
I touched it with outsiders' eyes,
Yet as a tiny child, spurred to tears
By one distorted image.

Amy Nithsdale

WARRIOR OF PEACE

As the darkness creeps across the sky,
A rare beauty fills the air,
It will create a feeling of tranquillity,
A feeling the whole world should share.

The wonder of seeing the highlands,
As the morning mist starts to rise,
The feeling of peace and joy in your heart,
Will bring the tears to your eyes.

You will stand and look in wonder,
As the pipers come in view,
When their haunting sound fills the air,
You feel they are playing to you.

Remembering that in years gone by,
These warriors roamed the lands,
Fighting for their true beliefs,
Your lives were in their hands.

Now time has healed the troubled lands
And peace and beauty live,
Enjoy this feeling of harmony,
That only Scotland can give.

Lesley Allen

CALEDONIA

The listening silence
echoes,
as the forest keeps life
squirreled
like nuts waiting future
wakening.
Underfoot summer's embers
lie squandered,
releasing needled fragrance
gifted
to wrap the morning in textured
headiness.
Moved, miserly clouds release
silvered shafts
burnishing green candled
pillars,
stalwarts of ancient precinct
minding time.
Drawn to the light, living things
look up
wondering beyond the canopy,
catching
the unsung melody of
beginnings.

Shirley Johnson

WAVE THE SALTIRE

Proud to be a Scot, Mon?
Aye, proud of it indeed!
Proud of our ancient history
When of our past we read.

The heroic blood of ancestors
Still pulses through our veins -
There's Wallace, Bruce and many more
And those very fiery Danes!

They have combined to make us
What we are today
And down throughout the ages
Have kept those Englishmen at bay!

The Scots have travelled far and wide
To every corner of the world,
So in every country you will find
The Scottish flag unfurled.

A feat of engineering? Aye,
You'll find a Scotsman there,
Because when all is said and done,
There's a brain beneath that bright red hair!

While Scott and Stevenson, of course,
Have used a pen in place of sword,
And Robbie Burns, *our* poet
Is by all of us adored.

Tough as our Highland cattle -
Aye, we're reared on porridge oats!
We've come down through the ages
By land, by sea and boats.

So, to our Saltire, white and blue,
Scotland! Here's a toast to you!

Joyce Hockley

LIFE'S LULLABY

Stars are peeping,
One by one,
Shadows deepen,
Day is done.

Today, I heard somebody laugh,
Somebody cried,
Today, a little child was born,
Somebody died.

The winter brings the frost and snow,
The roses die,
In summertime, they bloom again,
Their heads held high.

So sleep in peace my little one
And have no fear,
Life's not too bad when there's a smile,
For every tear.

Stars are peeping,
One by one,
Shadows deepen,
Day is done.

Matthew L Burns

PATRIARCH MACDONALD

I share the pain
O' this glen
Bearing witness in 'mind'
Tae Scots ill-fated men
Runnin' barefit
Clans scattered
Yon - the echoin' cry
Trapped energies - hauntin'
And Earth's passionate sighs
Humbly I pray in strange silence
While of forebears - do boast
For I - the line o' MacDonald
Must weep wi' their ghost.

Irene Gunnion
(nee MacDonald)

AND COMPELLING

A garden, where nature,
Deemed;
Creative village, genuine.

A proud land.
Bass rock, rising 107m,
Above the Scottish coast, near Edinburgh.
Long winters, and the fierce, North Sea.
The Scottish Highlands,
A region of mountains, and deep valleys.
Sparkling lakes, in the glens.
Southern uplands, region of rolling hills.

Scotch whisky, the patient treatment;
Of necessary course.

Bred of fertile lessons,
Character curious, and compelling;
Sir Walter Scott,
Scottish novelist, and poet, of the Romantic Period.
Robert Burns,
Scottish poet, and writer of traditional,
Scottish folk songs.

Not only in literature,
Has Scotland given to the world,
Bounty in spirit,
Scotch champion;
Engineering of renown,
Another, in fervour, Scottish.

Rowland Warambwa

This Is Scotland

Scotland is a great place to be,
The purple heather on the hills.
You can't beat a wee tot of Scotch whisky,
Scotland is really the best you see.

The thistle is the nation's emblem,
They say that Nessie the monster is seen
Swimming in Loch Ness, but a mystery
This tale still will be.

There are many tartans and the famous kilt
And sporran look so smart and neat.
The bagpipes make a unique sound,
As those who listen may have found.

The glens, the mountains, such lovely scenery,
The famous people that were brave and true.
Scotland is proud of its history,
So raise a glass of that Scotch whisky.

Jean Foster

SCOTLAND THE FAIR

I know each charging facet of her winter-painted face
raw sleet-gorged winds sweeping arctic white
ranks of spruce denying winter's shroud
bruised clouds above unsullied snow
I know the laughter of a madcap mountain stream
crystal clear and sharp with Celtic snow
tumbling breakneck to the glen

I know the budding tenderness of spring
a mist of bluebells 'neath the trees, fleet messengers of May
I know her glens when morning mist is rising
when pale light bleaches the slopes
and the sinuous road fades to distant hills
I know her drowsy days of summer's brief flirtation
the muted murmuring of bees beneath an azure sky

I know her face in autumn - nature running riot on her cheeks
plying an artist's brush in a thousand glorious hues
chestnut, hazel, tawny yellow, rust and amber
burnished copper, gold and bronze
I know when sunset turns her snow-capped hills to rose
and sends its rays to dip the mirrored loch
like shimmering fingers to a pot of molten gold

I know her towering heights and craggy cliffs
her brown-tinged cataracts plunging to the sea
her hidden caves once home to wolves and bears
I know the otter's song, the baying of a stag
the eagle's scream, the bark of a seal
I know the heady fragrance of peat fire smoke
at one with heather perfumed air

She is my jewel, my strength, my solace
She is my anchor when tempest's rage
She is my restoration,
In my mind I see her beauty and my soul knows peace
I am home.

Jan Whitfield

TO AN OIL RIG

Great tow'ring monstrous metal beastie,
Oh! Whit a throbbin's in thy breastie!
Nicht an' day, producin' joose -
That thick black oil, man puts tae use.

Ye staund there high on muckle pegs,
Reachin' tae the sky, like a dug that begs!
Whiles in the derkest winter nicht.
Ye shine like a thoosand diamonds bricht.

The whirlin' girdy brings the crew,
That sweat an' toil the long day through,
The life is hard when seas are rough,
It's true, they're 'made o' sterner stuff!'

The pumps ne'er stop, though the wild waves heave.
But workers look ahead to 'leave'
The oil might end up in oor cars,
The crew, they head for the nearest bars!

Catherine Buchan

Scotland

Scotland oh Scotland inviting and bright,
In all its splendour day or night.
Its beauty elsewhere I'm sure you won't find,
From John O'Groats to Land's End, it all stays in your mind.

The islands are glorious this has to be said,
Mull, Skye and Iona are simply the best!
The wildlife and beauty of the countryside so green,
Sunsets on Crinan just have to be seen.

Loch Fyne to Loch Lomond is such a treat,
The scenery would sweep you right off your feet.
Rain, hail or snow the best is Glencoe,
With its long winding road and its glorious sights,
So why not take a look and I'm sure you will find,
That Scotland will always live on in your mind.

Ryan Taylor

MY WOODPILE

There's a robin in my woodpile
Sitting on her nest so neat,
Made from moss and downy feathers -
Tireless work 'til it's complete.
Soon will hatch the tiny fledglings
Hidden well from prying eyes,
In a short while they'll be flying
And their home will be the skies.

There's a hedgehog in my woodpile
Rolled up snugly in the leaves,
There he sleeps all through the winter
Thankful for the warmth he feels.

Many think a woodpile's boring,
Trunks and branches cast aside,
But in mine there's much excitement,
Keeping record gives me pride.

Children play around my woodpile
And their laughter fills the air,
Hide-and-seek and catch the bean-bag
Are the games that they all share.

Landing on my woodpile branches
Butterflies of lovely hue,
Insects, moths and once a grass snake
Slithered silently from view.

On the topmost branch, a blackbird
Often sings her morning song
And a field mouse darts to cover
Hiding in the grasses long.

Every day there's something different,
Things that others do not see,
There's much life in my old woodpile
Bringing lots of joy to me.

Glenys Moses

A TRIBUTE

Who is Anne Miller
A fellow poet I have gathered
Well! To her I owe a poetic debt
For Robert Burns' name first said 'Hi' to me
While reading an article 'Ceud Mile Failte'
Yes Anne Miller visited Scotland
Yes again she had a brill time
Her story she shared in the Poet Corner magazine
Robert's life story was told all over again
Me a young poet was honoured
To learn such great lessons
They say a true poet never dies
While reading Anne's article
This came to life once again
Robert Burns must be singing in heaven
For here on earth he has a worthy clan.

Carolie Pemberton

MY DAD
(Died April 5th 1979)

He was a very private man
He always wore a suit
And never took his coat off
In the house
He never laughed out loud
Or argued in the street
In company he hardly spoke
A really introverted bloke
He never took me on his knee
He never dandled me
Or held me upside down
Or swung me on his shoulders
When he took me for a walk
I had to run
To keep up to his stride
We never had a car
In which to ride
A lot of things
He never did
That dads do nowadays
But when he died
In my turn
I never felt
Anything
But
Devastation

Alan Harry Francis

A Sister I Adore

Lonely now you're just a dream
Of days we used to share
I still hear your laughter
Although no longer there
The telephone is silent
Your weekly call no more
But memories still live on
Of a sister I adore.

I think of days we used to walk
When we were very small
Holding hands as darkness fell
Frightened by it all
Still I see your smiling face
When I close my eyes
You come to me as I sleep
From God's heaven in the skies.

Florence Davies

HAME

Each day so different.
From high, boiling seas
crashing, searching for shore.
To golden, pink sunsets
as background to
dolphin school, leaping and playing.

To lie at night as the wind
howls and screams across the velux
above my bed, is a lullaby
like no other.

To stroll along the foreshore
or by the harbour, exchanging greetings.
'Fit like,' 'Aye, aye,'
From one and all.
Not this in the city.

'Here a' ken yer bisness afore yersel'
Why not?
We are here for each other
as and when we are needed.

I do not need the mansion grand
that a lottery win would bring
to improve the pleasure
of living by the Moray Firth.

Dalziel

THE GIFT OF LIFE

The gift of life is precious,
We must never let it go.
We are put on this earth for many things
What counts are the deeds we do.

We raise our family as best we can,
Give them love and tender care,
Listen to their hopes and worries,
Always have time to spare.

Time also to spare for all our friends
Who are special in every way.
Share all their troubles, all their joys,
Give them help from day to day.

This road we travel seems long some days,
Full of things that seem hard to bear.
Then someone appears to lend a hand,
Our heart lifts when we know they are there.

When you lay your head on the pillow each night,
Close your eyes and offer a prayer.
A prayer of thanks to God above,
Because we know that he really cares.

Turn to him in your darkest hour,
Whether your *worry* is big or small.
Then God in his wisdom will answer your prayer,
With love and compassion for all.

Babe Morgan

GUARDIAN ANGEL

In my darkness you watch me sleeping
In my dream your light is peeping
In my silence your hand it falls
In my sorrow your smile it calls
In my darkness you watch me sleeping
You rescue my tears when I am weeping.

Rebecca Punter

MEMORIES

Looking back along the years,
Remembering, our hopes and fears,
Grief and sadness, filled the nation,
Joyous times, and great elation.
Love and romance, that we shared,
We both knew, how much we cared.
Happy times we spent together,
Caring not for wind or weather.
Marriage children, family life,
Caused a lot of stress and strife!
Through the years, we battled on,
Even though your health had gone.
Ever hoping for improvement -
Things got worse -
With much less movement.
Aches and pains, and lots of moaning,
What a life!
We all kept groaning.
Happy days and happy nights,
In-between the stress and strife!
So suddenly your life has gone,
And I am left, to battle on.

Rose E Selby

The Brilliance Of Dawn

Clouds of grey waiting to disperse
Hanging heavy upon red rooftops
Dull meaningless ironic of life
Darkness beckoning enfolding the day
The world dormant, creation almost without life
Dawn bursts in, its way led by a radiance of crystal
The grey hanging cloud dispersing its secret
Unleashing a sparkle of creation
Like sugar covering a cake
White diamonds upon the crust of the earth
The ground yielding to this covering
Allowing itself to be clothed
Covering the red of the rooftops
In white in the purity, the innocence of nature
Rooftops covered no red showing
Only freshly fallen snow
Pure untouched formed out of God
The jewel of his element
The irony of life to live not die
To have light not darkness
His son the glory of the dawn
The diamond that sparkles the crystal of nature
His creation covered by the cloth of God
Made pure made beautiful
Sparkling like the glory of the morning
The radiance of the day.

Belinda J Howells

IT'S THE THOUGHT THAT COUNTS

There's a knock on the door, the postman's out there
holding a parcel high up in the air.
Who is it from? What is inside?
Hurry and get all those tight knots untied.

Why waste the time to untie the knots
bring a sharp knife to put in the slots,
tearing the paper, opening the box,
it's all full of packing, secure, like Fort Knox.

Inside the large box was the one smaller beside,
all wrapped in silver with pink ribbon tied,
attached to this box was a letter stuck on,
with simple words written, 'From your loving son.'

'This gift is so special, one you'll never see
the reason it's special, it's to you from me,
whenever you're lonely or just feeling blue,
you've only to hold it, I'll be thinking of you.
Please never unwrap it, just leave ribbon tied,
hold the box to your heart, it's love that's inside.'

Leslie Holgate

DO WE CARE?

Do we care that in a far country
They leave unwanted female babies to die?
Because she is female, they think of no use
She is subject to the worst abuse
Because of a rule, of one child only
And she is left to die so lonely.
A helpless child, human greed
Call it what you may, there's no excuse
Do *they* belong to the Human Race?
And do *they*, deserve a place?
Do we care?

Cloe Wilton

A FOOTBALL LEGEND

When you think of Scottish heroes there are many you can name
But my own choice would be Stirling's favourite son.
His exploits on the football field confirm his claim to fame
And are epitomised by the trophies which he won.

Apart from his ability upon the soccer pitch
He had a will to win and a football brain
And his qualities of leadership were so very rich
That he made a unique contribution to the game.

As a soccer wizard he was gifted with all the tricks
And he gave his all in every game he played.
Although small in stature - he was only five feet six -
But, personality-wise, no one put him in the shade.

In the 60s and 70s, in his Leeds United days
And captaining Scotland in arguably its best hour,
He was the linchpin of the teams in so many ways
And the piston which provided skill and power.

No doubt, you will have guessed the name of my hero
For in his chosen sport he always gave his all.
Billy Bremner is the legendary redheaded dynamo
For whom football was life and life, football!

John W Skepper